United States Navy

FOR KIDS

by Eric Z

Text © 2017 Eric Z.of www.TheKidsBooks.Blogspot.com

The Z KIDS BOOKS
www.thekidsbooks.blogspot.com

All rights reserved

All images CC-BY-3.0:

This file is a work of a sailor or employee of the U.S. Navy, taken or made as part of that person's official duties. As a work of the U.S. federal government, the image is in the public domain.

This file has been identified as being free of known restrictions under copyright law, including all related and neighboring rights.

Except for Sammy the Seal who is exclusively owned and cared for by ©Eric Z:

That's me!

Your Free Gift

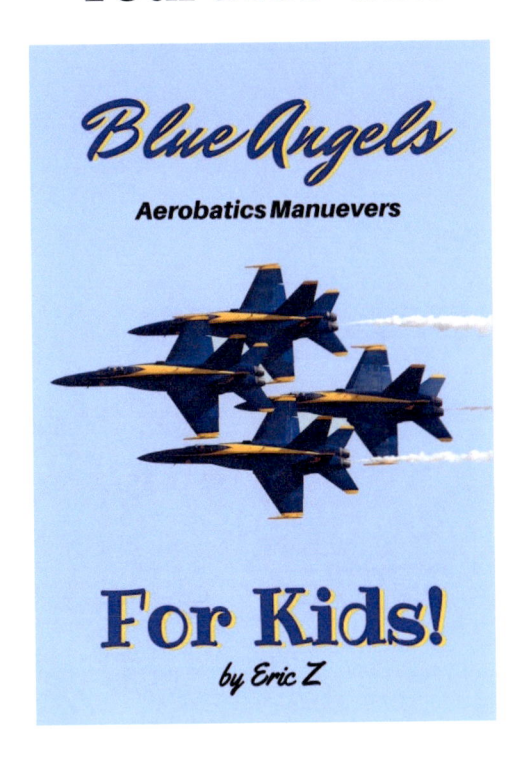

Get the Blue Angels Aerobatics for FREE

When you join The Kids Books!
Just type this in any web browser:

bit.ly/aeroGift

To all the kids who want to be a NAVY Pilot

If you persist, you will succeed!

Table of Contents

United States Navy Pilot 1

Your Free Gift 3

Joining the United States Navy 6

Flight School 9

Carrier Operations 12

    Landing Approach 17

    Flight Deck Crew 22

No Fly Zones and Air Superiority 24

Anti-Aircraft Missiles 31

Ground Support and Attack 33

Supersonic Flight 38

    Vortices 40

The US Navy's Aircraft Fleet 42

    FIGHTERS 42

        Grumman F-14 Tomcat - the top gun fighter! 42

        McDonnell Douglas F/A-18 Hornet 47

        Boeing F/A-18E/F Super Hornet 50

        Lockheed Martin F-35 Lightning II 53

    RECONNAISSANCE and ECM AIRCRAFT 57

        Northrop Grumman E-2 Hawkeye 57

        Northrop Grumman EA-6B Prowler 58

        Boeing EA-18G Growler 59

    RESCUE AND MULTI-ROLE AIRCRAFT 60

        Sikorsky CH-53E Super Stallion / MH-53 Sea Dragon 60

        Sikorsky SH-60 Seahawk 61

Your Free Gift 64

Joining the United States Navy

Your journey to becoming a United States Naval Aviator, and Navy Pilot, actually starts NOW.

In school you must strive to get the best grades, and do your very best in all of your classes.

On top of that you must always try to be the best person you can be. The United States Navy gets a lot of people, everyday, who want to be a TOP GUN pilot, and they only take the best.

And on top of that, you must STAY CLEAN, and never get arrested or get in trouble. The Armed Forces do not take anyone with a criminal record!

To join the Navy you must be:
- At least 18 years old
- A United States Citizen
- Have NO criminal record

The Navy also has STRICT physical fitness and EYESIGHT tests for pilots. When you join the Navy, make sure to talk to your RECRUITER about these specific pilot tests.

Before you become a pilot, you must become an OFFICER. This is also called a "commissioned officer."

To become an officer, you must go to COLLEGE and get at least a four year degree called a BACHELOR'S DEGREE.

US NAVY — You gotta go to College kids!

But the cool part is: The Navy will help you get a Bachelor's Degree!

The NROTC, Naval Reserve Officers Training Corps:

When you join the NROTC, you go to college and earn your degree, at the same time you are already in the Navy. But more important: The Navy will also help you pay for your college tuition. After you are done with the NROTC you will be enlisted in the Navy as an ENSIGN.

Navy Officer Ranks and Insignia

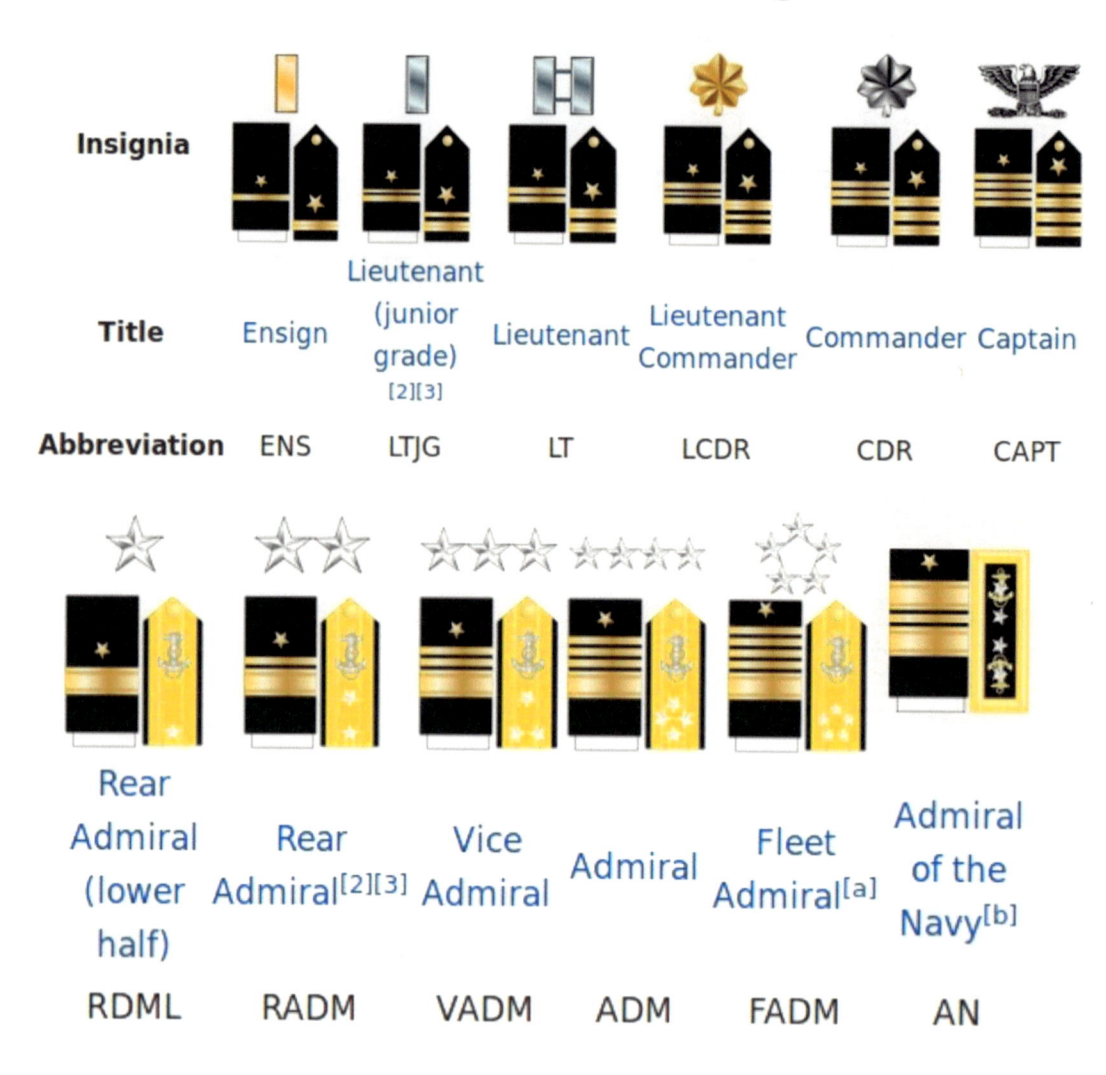

Insignia						
Title	Ensign	Lieutenant (junior grade)[2][3]	Lieutenant	Lieutenant Commander	Commander	Captain
Abbreviation	ENS	LTJG	LT	LCDR	CDR	CAPT

Rear Admiral (lower half)	Rear Admiral[2][3]	Vice Admiral	Admiral	Fleet Admiral[a]	Admiral of the Navy[b]
RDML	RADM	VADM	ADM	FADM	AN

Once you are done with college, and have your four year degree, you must also go to OCS: Officer Candidate School. Here you will continue your education and learn to be an officer of the United States Navy. Only then can you continue finally to...

8

Flight School

The basics of flying are learned first. The United States Navy and the Air Force both learn to fly with the T6 Texan aircraft. This takes about six months:

Beechcraft T-6 Texan II

When you are done with this primary flight training, the ADVANCED training begins. The Navy has a lot of different aircraft, so after this school you will decide which aircraft TYPE to fly:

- Multi engine aircraft - Cargo and patrol aircraft
- Rotary winged aircraft - Helicopters
- Fixed wing aircraft - Jet fighters!

If you have chosen the Jet Fighter path, your next stop is "Tailhook training" with the T-45 Goshawk:

Here you will learn the most difficult part of being a Navy pilot, and why Navy pilots are the best in the world: Taking off and landing on an aircraft carrier!

This advanced training lasts 23 weeks, after which you are QUALIFIED as a Naval Aviator and you receive your pilot's wings!

Launch and Recovery training aboard the USS Harry Truman

The coveted pilot's wings!

I prefer the badge

Carrier Operations

All aircraft on the aircraft carrier are launched with the STEAM CATAPULT:

This is what it looks like for the pilot:

A shooter gives the signal to launch an F/A-18:

F/A 18F Super Hornet of the Jolly Rogers of Strike Fighter Squadron (VFA) 103 launching with the steam catapult:

The aircraft take off with maximum thrust and FULL AFTERBURNER. The afterburner makes the flames as this F-14 takes off:

F-18 taking off with full afterburner

Take Off!

F/A-18C Hornet, assigned to the "Golden Dragons" of Strike Fighter Squadron One Nine Two (VFA-192), launches from the flight deck of the USS Kitty Hawk.

Here we go!

After the pilots fly their mission, it's time to land; this is the hardest part!
When seen from the air, the aircraft carrier looks very small. Some pilots say that trying to land on an aircraft carrier at sea, is like trying to land on a potato-chip!

Modern Aircraft Carriers have Angled Flight Decks:

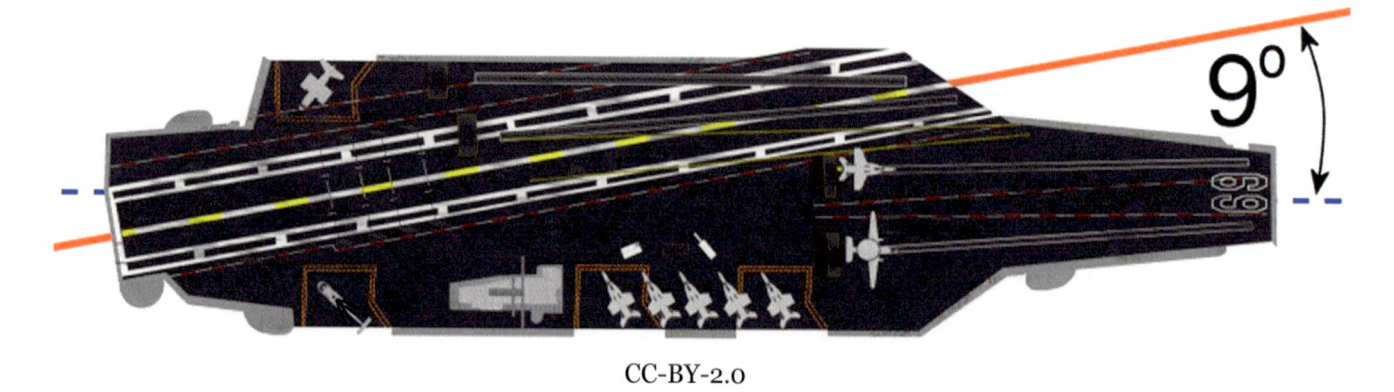

CC-BY-2.0

This way two or more planes can take off and land at the same time.

Go to http://thekidsbooks.blogspot.com/ to see this as an animation!

Landing Approach

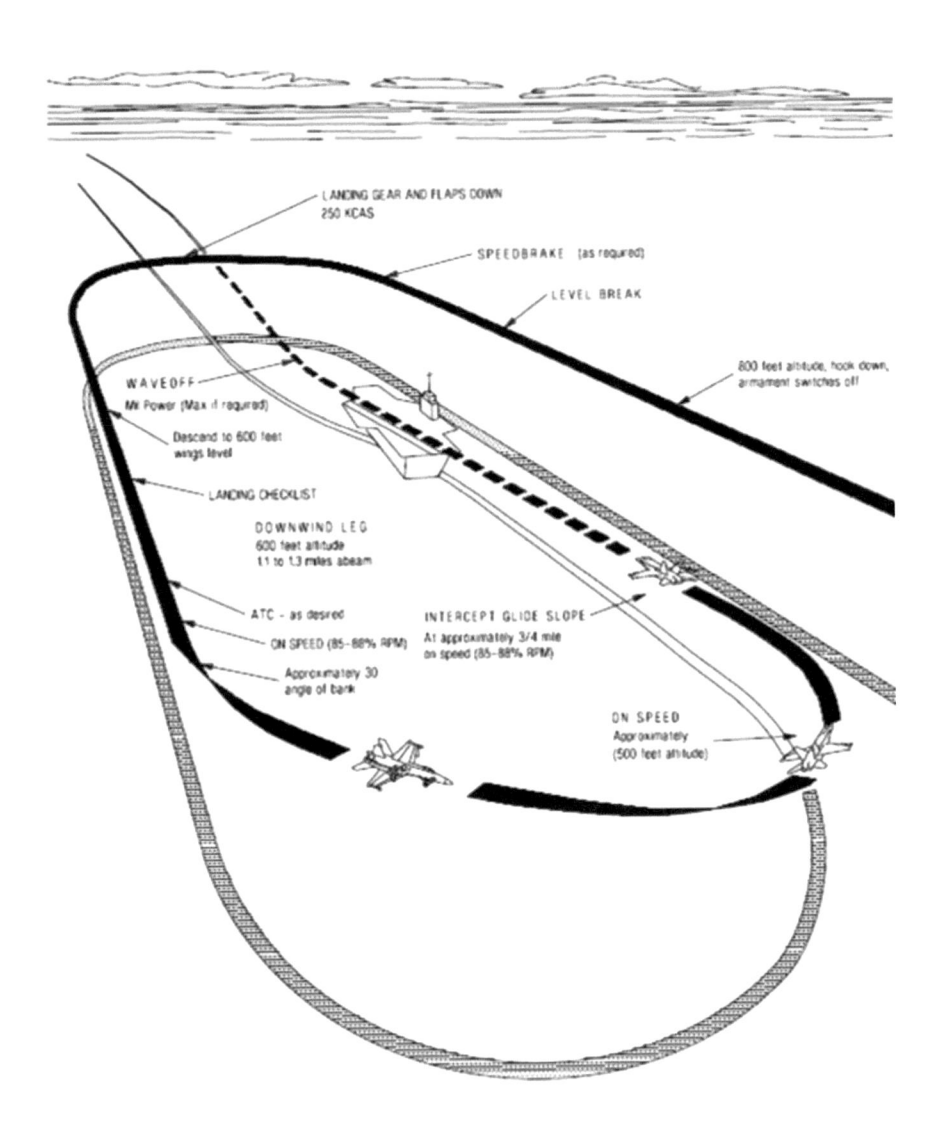

The pilot must fly his aircraft around the aircraft carrier and then into position. This is called "final approach".

He has to make the final approach perfect in order to land on the aircraft carrier safely!

F-18 Hornet on final approach:

The tailhook can be clearly seen on this F-18 coming in for landing:

The most challenging part; catching the WIRE. There are three or four wires depending on which Aircraft Carrier you are landing on…

Below you can see three wires in the landing zone of the aircraft carrier:

If the tail hook does not catch a wire, the pilot must apply FULL AFTERBURNER and take off again!

A Successful Landing!

You can see an awesome video of real aircraft carrier operations at The KidsBooks, **just type this into any browser:**

bit.ly/2mCarrier

Who needs a tailhook?

The flight deck of an aircraft carrier is VERY BUSY!

In this picture of the Harry S. Truman aircraft carrier you can see an F-18 taking off from the front, and the F-18 in the middle is going to its parking spot. The wings are folded up so the F-18 will fit better on the busy deck of the aircraft carrier.

ALL aircraft on an aircraft carrier have folding wings:

Flight Deck Crew

Pilots must pay special attention to the flight deck crew.

They do everything from FUEL the aircraft, to load its weapons and fix the aircraft when it is broken. Also very important, the ground crew is ready to put out any fires and take care of any emergencies that can happen on deck.

Flying would be impossible without the flight deck crew!

The Flight Deck Crew wear colored jackets to identify themselves:

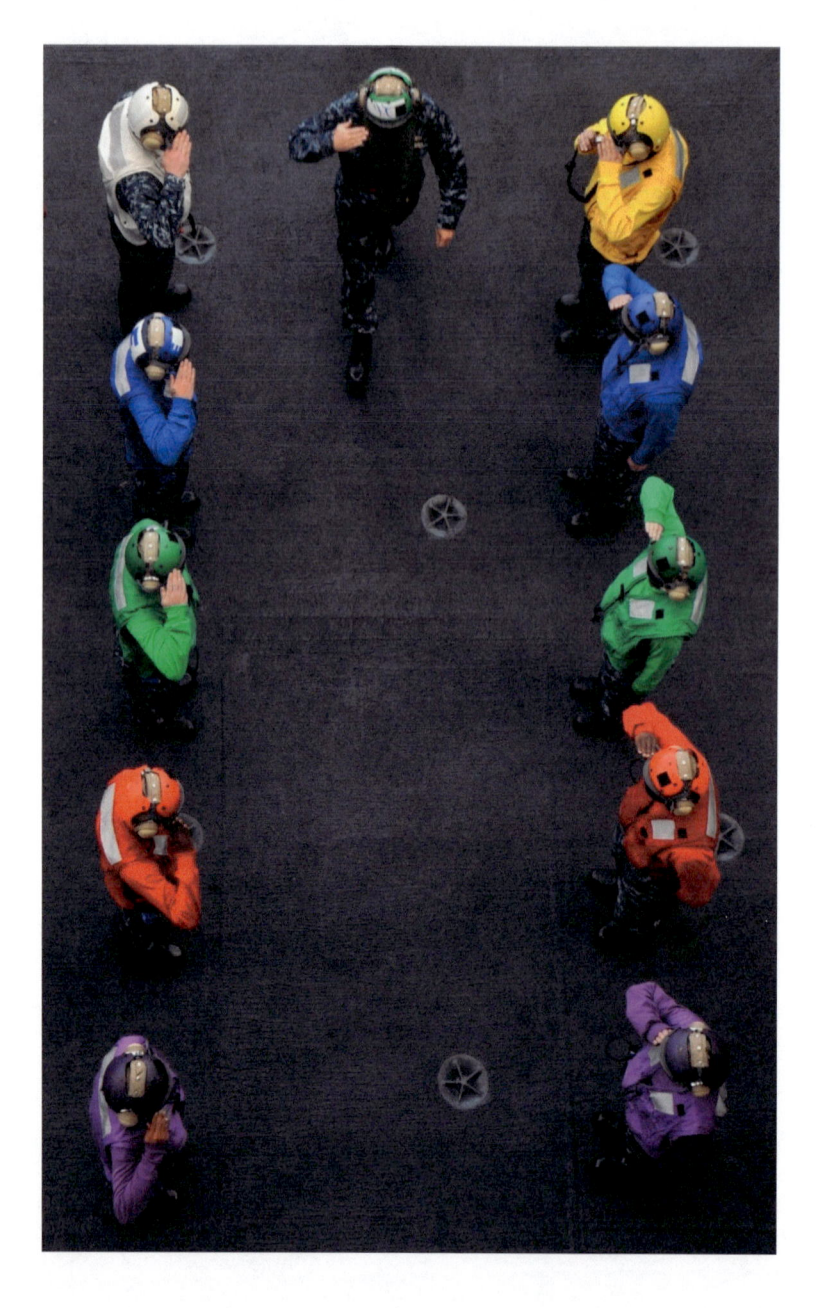

22

- **Landing Signal Officers (white)** — help the pilots land their aircraft.
- **Catapult Crew** — Also called "Shooters" Control the Steam Catapult and launch the aircraft.
- **Ordnance men** — load the bombs and bullets!
- **Aviation Fuel Handlers** — refuel the planes…
- **Plane Captains** — are the LEAD MECHANICS and take care of the planes.
- **Plane Handlers** — move the aircraft above and below deck and into position.
- **Flight Deck Crew** — Do EVERYTHING else!
- **Aircrew** — the pilots! They don't have a special color, although their flight suite and G-suit are dark green.

Here we see a Marines pilot in a light brown flight suite with the dark green G-suit on top. Marine pilots are also NAVAL AVIATORS and undergo the same training in the same flight school as Navy Pilots.

No Fly Zones and Air Superiority

One of the first things the United States Navy must do in an enemy warzone is to establish a NO FLY ZONE.

The US Navy does this of course with an aircraft carrier! This means the aircraft carrier will monitor the sky with RADAR, and the fighter aircraft will patrol the sky for enemy aircraft.

Any enemy aircraft found in this No Fly Zone will be shot down! The pilots of the US Navy will engage in "Air Combat Maneuvers" — this is also known as DOG FIGHTING.

The main goal during dogfighting is to get behind the enemy aircraft. This is known as "getting his six"; because on a clock, the Six O'Clock position is the same as the rear part of an aircraft.

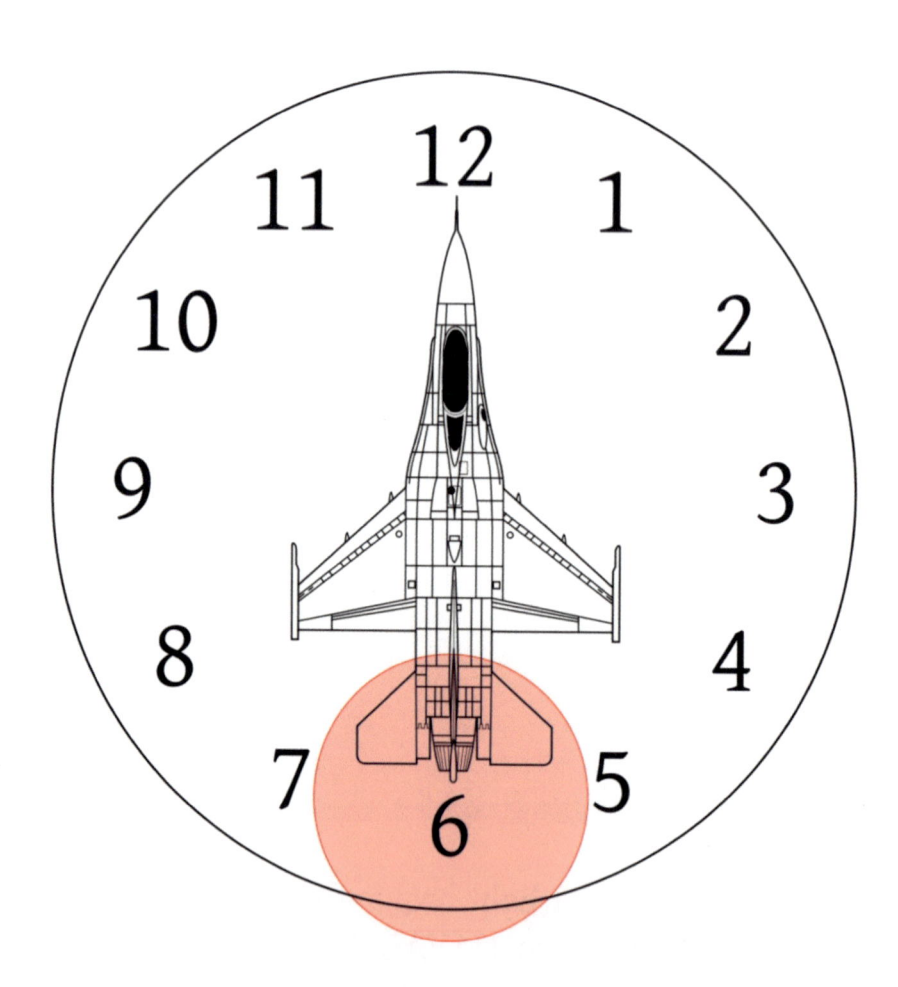

Air Combat Maneuvers are used to turn inside the enemy aircraft and "get his six".

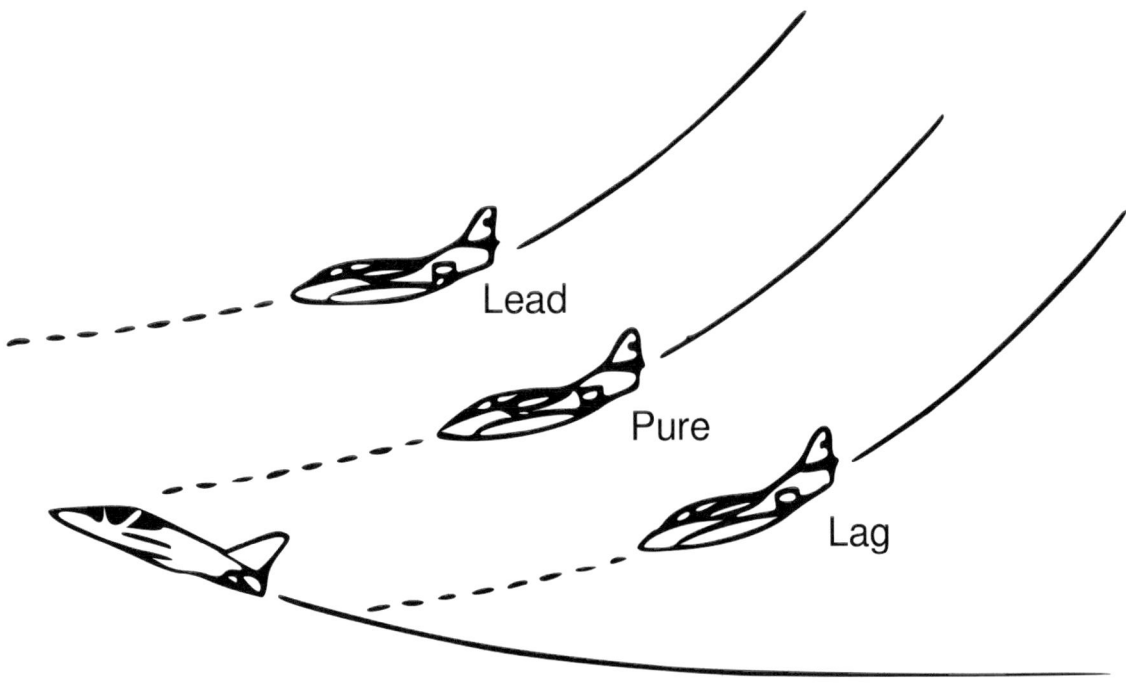

But air combat is 3 dimensional; climbing and diving are just as important as turning:

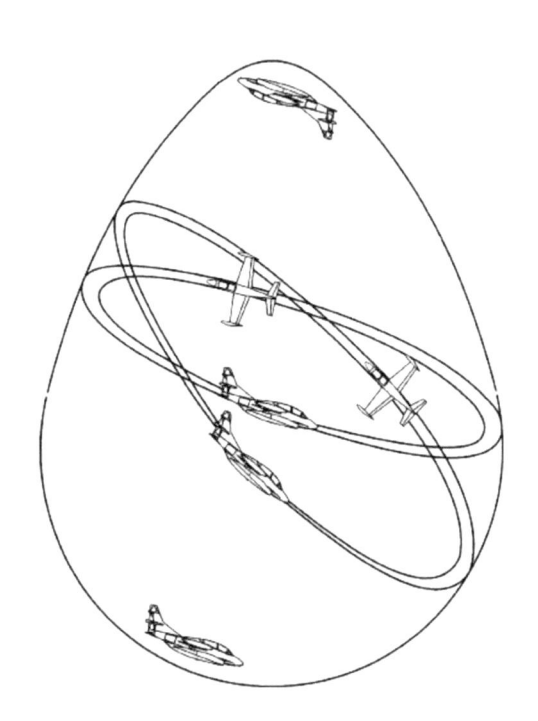

The early phase of Air Combat; neither pilot has an advantage, and neither one of them is in position to fire his cannon or anti-aircraft missiles:

An A4 Skyhawk tries to turn inside an F-14 Tomcat during Air Combat Training over China Lake California.

Now the A4 Skyhawk has the F-14 Tomcat's SIX in his sights, the perfect position to fire his cannon or launch an air-to-air anti-aircraft missile!

An F/A-18 Hornet takes on an F5E Tiger AND a Dassault Mirage!

An F-16 and an F-14 maneuvering to get the other's 6 O'clock: position!

This F-14 Tomcat has the F-5E Tiger's SIX, the perfect position to score a kill!

Once you are behind your enemy, you fire your cannon or launch an ANTI-AIRCRAFT MISSILE immediately!

FIRE!!!

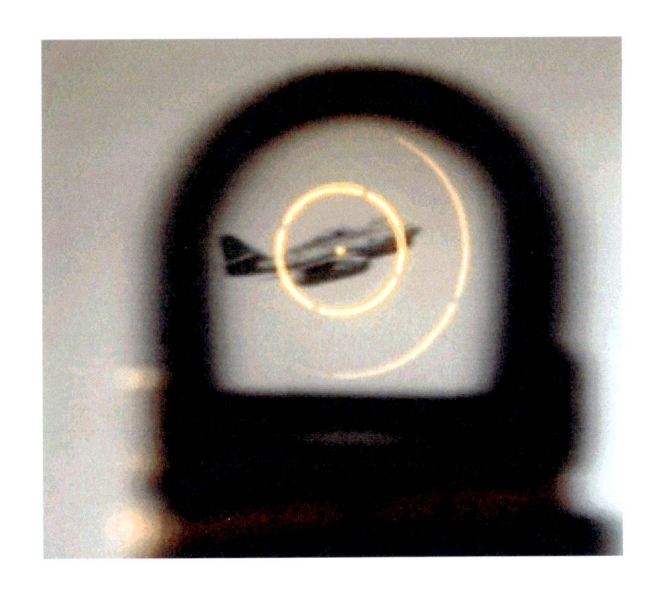

And this is what a real "kill" looks like for the pilot:

An F-105D Thunderchief shoots down a Mig-17 over Viet Nam

Anti-Aircraft Missiles

The AIM-9 Sidewinder is a heat-seeking missile, which means it locks onto the heat of the enemy aircraft's engine. Then it follows this heat all the way to the target—the enemy aircraft! This one is blue, which means it is a PRACTICE missile, with no explosives in it.

This one is NOT blue! An F-18 launches an AIM-9 sidewinder heat-seeking anti-aircraft missile.

The AIM-120 AMRAAM is a RADAR GUIDED missile.

AMRAAM = Advanced Medium-Range Air-to-Air Missile.

It is also "Fire and Forget"; because this missile has its own ACTIVE RADAR. Which means after the pilot fires it, it uses its own radar to follow and hit the target — the enemy aircraft! This enables to the pilot to maneuver for the next attack, without having to follow his own missile.

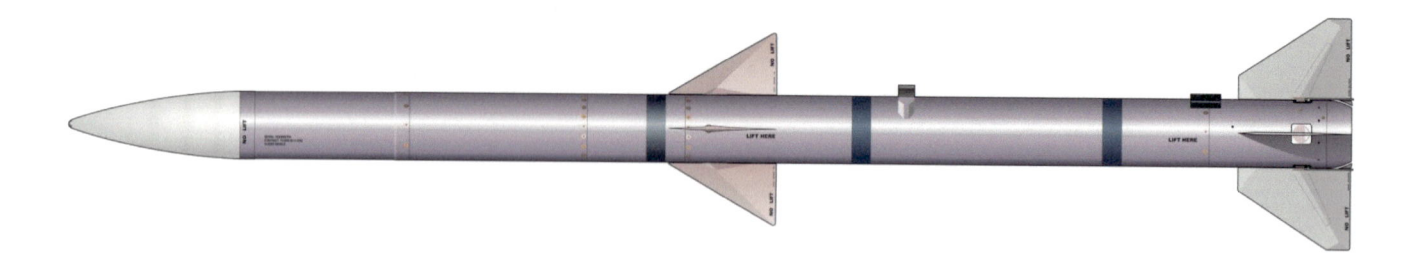

An F-18 launches an AIM-120 AMRAAM Radar Guided anti-aircraft missile:

Ground Support and Attack

Once Air Superiority has been achieved, and the No Fly Zone has been cleared, the fighter pilots can now concentrate on "Ground Support". This means supporting the troops on the ground, by destroying enemy targets like: tanks, bunkers, artillery, or enemy buildings.

A U.S. Navy McDonnell F-4B Phantom II of Fighter Squadron VF-111 Sundowners drops 227 kg Mk 82 bombs over Vietnam during 1971.

An F4U Corsair fires its ZUNI missiles on a run against a Japanese stronghold on Okinawa in World War Two:

The Zuni rockets in the photo above are "UNguided" missiles.

Much better are "guided" missiles, which can be steered or guided all the way to the target to ensure a 100% kill ratio!

The AGM-65 Maverick is a guided AIR TO GROUND missile, and it is *REALLY BAD NEWS* for tanks!

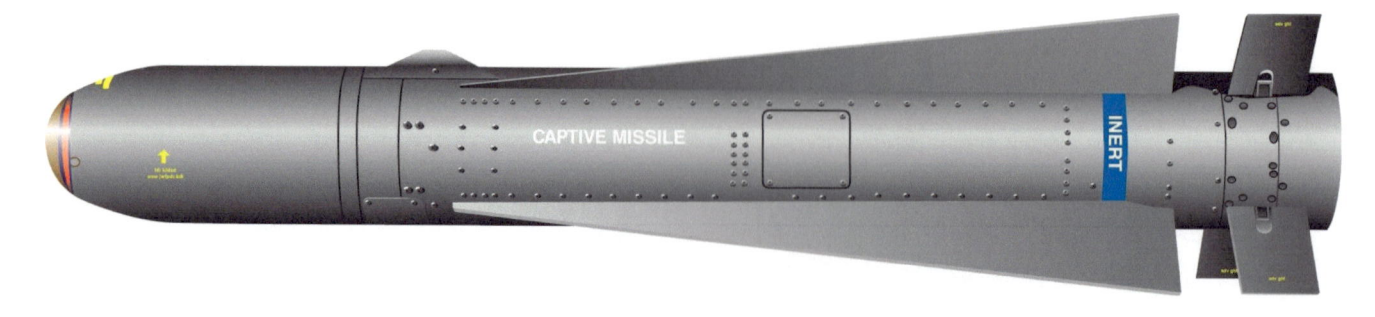

AGM-65 Maverick Air to Ground Guided Missile

F/A-18C Hornet armed with an AGM-65 Maverick over Iraq

The Maverick can be guided by the pilot, from the aircraft, or from someone else on the ground who is "marking" the target with a LASER ILLUMINATOR:

The Navy SEAL on the right is marking the target while his buddy on the left covers him.

Once the target has been acquired, or marked, the pilot can launch the Maverick and it will lock onto the target with deadly accuracy!

The aftermath of a Maverick attack: An Iraqi Type 59 tank lies in ruins after an allied attack during Operation Desert Storm:

An Iraqi Type 69 main battle tank burns during Operation Desert Storm.

Supersonic Flight

SUPERSONIC means faster than the speed of sound.

When an aircraft flies faster than the speed of sound, SHOCK WAVES are formed.

These shockwaves form areas above the wings, and around the aircraft with very low air pressure.

The air pressure can be so low, that the moisture in the air actually comes out, and looks like steam.

This is also called VAPOR.

The vapor shows you the actual shock waves in this photo of an F/A-18C:

When the shock waves form around the entire aircraft, this is also called a VAPOR CONE.

Vortices

The swirling vapors coming off of the wings, and above the fuselage in this photo are called VORTICES.

Vortices usually form on the wingtips and at the front of the wings and fuselage. The MOISTURE in the air comes out because of the very low pressure of the air in the vortice. This is the same effect of the supersonic shock waves and vapor cones.

Supersonic flight, Vortices, and Vapor Cones are cool!

The US Navy's Aircraft Fleet

FIGHTERS

Grumman F-14 Tomcat - the top gun fighter!

The F-14 Tomcat was the Navy's premier fighter plane, the TOP GUN aircraft, and air superiority fighter until the newer F-18 replaced it.

The F-14 has SWING WINGS. This means that the pilot can move the wings forwards or backwards during flight.

In the next photos, the wings are swept forward for take-off and landing, and low speed maneuvers...

An F-14A Tomcat of fighter squadron VF-84: The Jolly Rogers.

F-14 firing the AIM-54 Phoenix Radar Guided Anti-Aircraft Missile

When the F-14 pilot wants to fly faster, he sweeps the wings backwards. Swept back wings enable the plane to fly faster—even faster than the speed of sound!

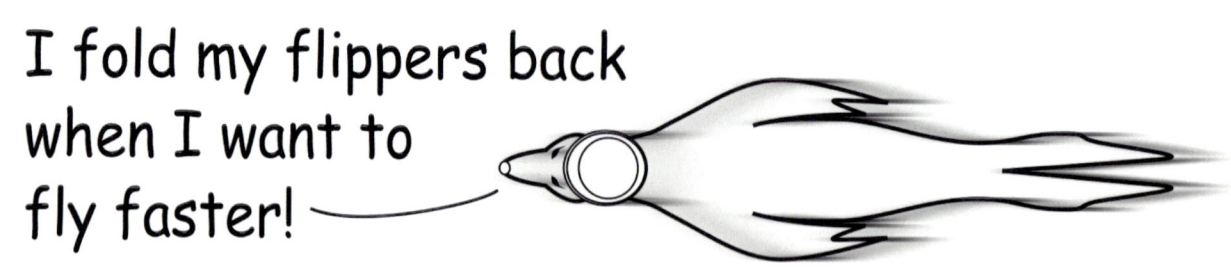

I fold my flippers back when I want to fly faster!

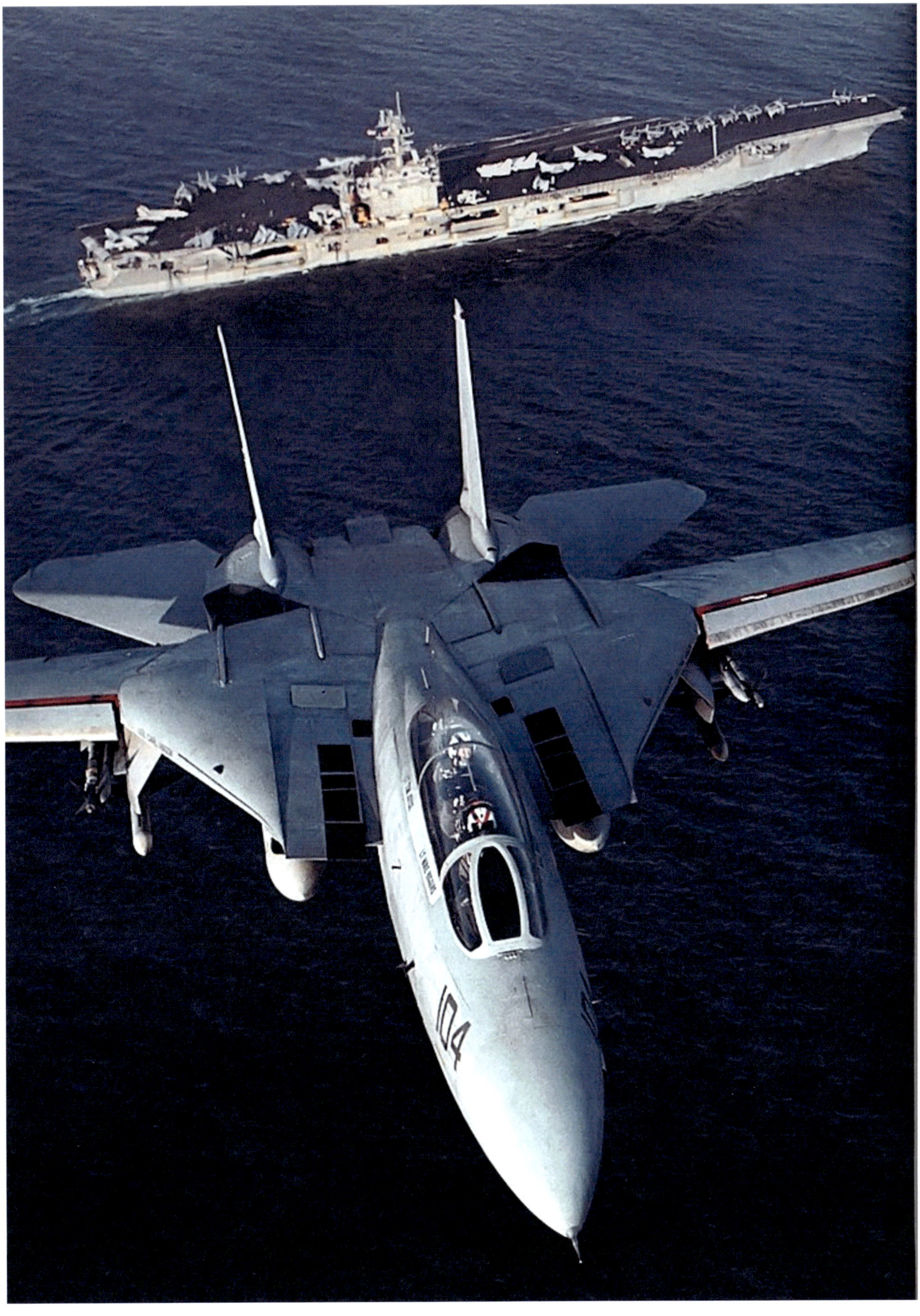

F-14 Tomcat General characteristics
Crew: 2 (Pilot and Radar Intercept Officer)
Length: 62 ft 9 in
Wingspan: *Spread:* 64 ft *Swept:* 38 ft
Height: 16 ft
Empty weight: 43,735 lb (19,838 kg)
Powerplant: 2 × General Electric F110-GE-400 afterburning turbofans
Dry thrust: 16,610 lbf each
Thrust with afterburner: 28,200 lbf each

Performance
Maximum speed: Mach 2.34 : 1,544 mph, at high altitude
Service ceiling: 50,000+ ft
Rate of climb: >45,000 ft/min
Thrust/weight: 0.88 (1.0 with loaded weight & 50% internal fuel)

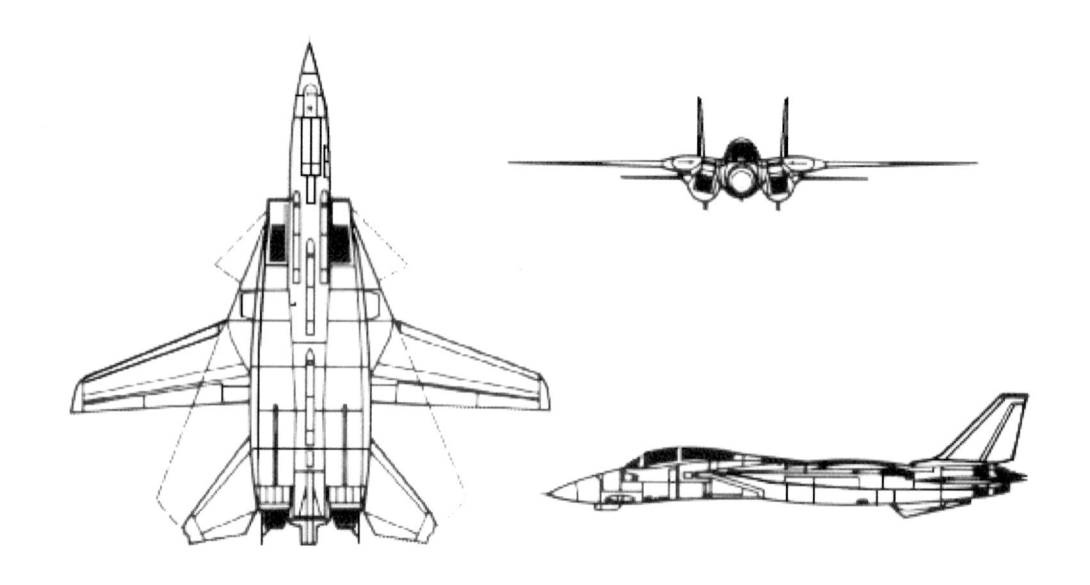

The F-14 Tomcat was an AWESOME aircraft, and the pilots loved it. After an amazing life in the United States Navy, the F-14 was retired in 2006 and replaced by the...

McDonnell Douglas F/A-18 Hornet

F-18 with a Laser Guided Bomb under its wing, and an AIM-9 Sidewinder on its wingtip.

F-18 carrying extra fuel tanks:

An F-18 showing off a full load of weapons:

F-18 General Characteristics
Crew: F/A-18C: 1, F/A-18D: 2 (pilot and weapons system officer)
Length: 56 ft
Wingspan: 40 ft
Height: 15 ft 4 in
Empty weight: 23,000 lb
Loaded weight: 36,970 lb
Powerplant: 2 × General Electric F404-GE-402 turbofans
Dry thrust: 11,000 lbf each
Thrust with afterburner: 17,750 lbf each

Performance
Maximum speed:
High altitude: Mach 1.8: 1,190 mph at 40,000 ft
Low altitude: Mach 1.2: 915 mph
Range: 1,089 nmi (1,250 miles, 2,000 km) with only two AIM-9s
Combat radius: 400 nmi (460 mi (740 km)) on air-air mission
Ferry range: 1,800 nmi (2,070 mi (3,330 km)
Service ceiling: 50,000 ft (15,240 m)
Rate of climb: 50,000 ft/min (254 m/s)
Wing loading: 93 lb/ft² (454 kg/m²)
Thrust/weight: 0.96 (1.13 with loaded weight & 50% internal fuel)

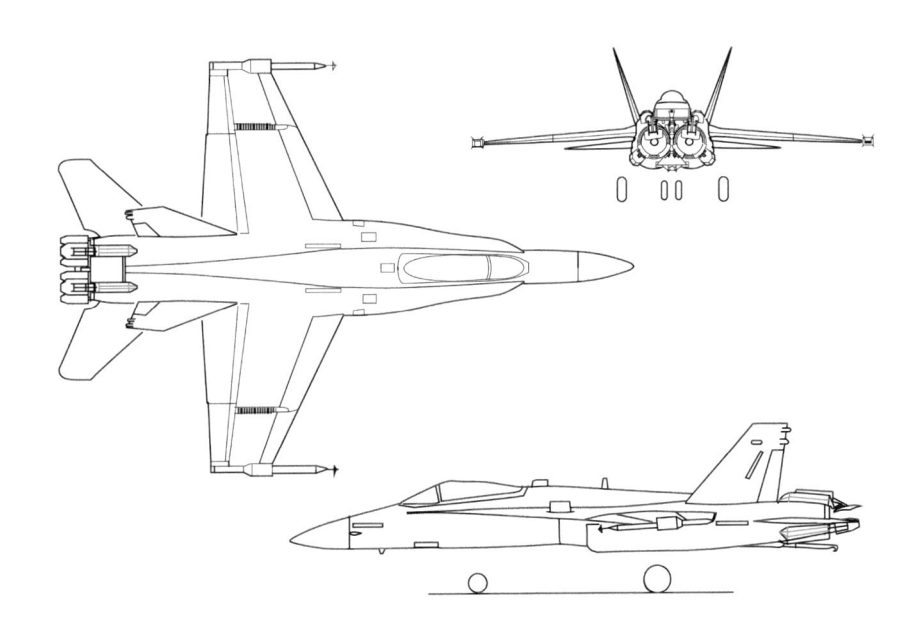

Boeing F/A-18E/F Super Hornet

The Super Hornet is bigger than the original F-18 Hornet. It can also fly farther, and carry more weapons, which is a big advantage for a fighter aircraft.

F/A-18E Single Seat Version

F/A-18F Two Seat Version

Two seater version of F/A-18 with an AGM-56 Maverick under its wing and an AIM-9 Sidewinder on its wingtip.

F-18 General Charcteristics
Crew: F/A-18E: 1, F/A-18F: 2
Length: 60 ft 1¼ in
Wingspan: 44 ft 8½ in
Height: 16 ft
Empty weight: 32,081 lb
Powerplant: 2 × General Electric F414-GE-400 turbofans
Dry thrust: 13,000 lbf each
Thrust with afterburner: 22,000 lbf each

Performance
Maximum speed: Mach 1.8 at 40,000 ft
Range: 1,275 nmi clean plus two AIM-9s
Service ceiling: 50,000+ ft
Rate of climb: 44,882 ft/min
Thrust/weight: 0.93 (1.1 with loaded weight & 50% internal fuel)

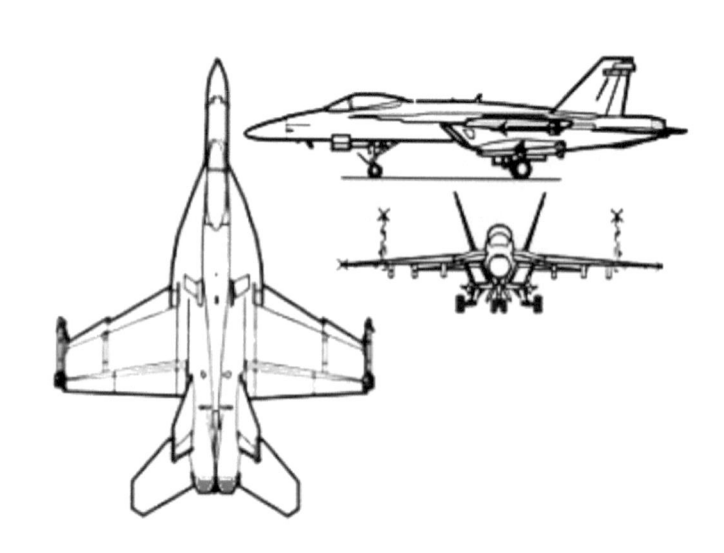

Lockheed Martin F-35 Lightning II

The Lockheed Martin F-35 Lightning II (Lightning two) is the newest addition to the U.S. Navy's fleet. The United States Navy, Air Force and Marines all have their own different version of the Lightning.

- F-35**A**: The Air Force version is the fastest.
    - It is also the only version with the GAU-22 inboard 25mm cannon.
- F-35**B**: The Marines version can take of vertically like a helicopter.
    - It can take off from anywhere, even in rough battlefields.
- F-35**C**: The Navy version has the biggest wings.
    - It can carry more weapons, more fuel, and fly farther.

A Navy F-35C with the larger folding wings:

One of the most important parts of the F-35 is its ADVANCED WEAPONS SYSTEM. The F-35 Helmet Mounted Display enables the pilot to engage multiple targets and launch missiles all while flying the aircraft. This gives him the decisive advantage in air combat.

The F-35B has an engine driven fan in the middle of the aircraft, and the exhaust nozzle can be pointed downwards. This enables the F-35 to take of vertically:

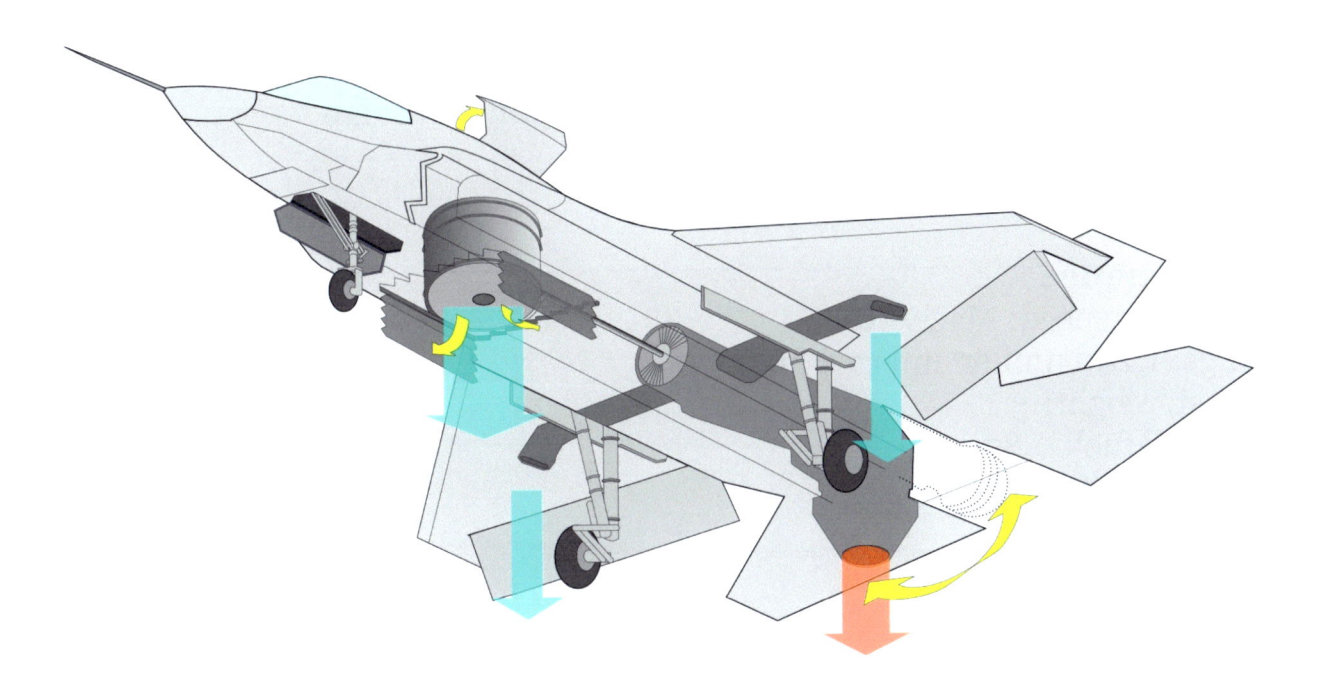

The F-35B taking off VERTICALLY from an aircraft carrier:

F-35 General characteristics
Crew: 1
Length: 50.5 ft
Wingspan: 35 ft
Height: 14.2 ft
Empty weight: 29,098 lb
Powerplant: 1 × Pratt & Whitney F135 afterburning turbofan
Dry thrust: 28,000 lbf
Thrust with afterburner: 43,000 lbf

Performance
Maximum speed: Mach 1.6+
Range: 1,200 nmi on internal fuel
Thrust/weight:
With full fuel: 0.87
With 50% fuel: 1.07

RECONNAISSANCE and ECM AIRCRAFT

Northrop Grumman E-2 Hawkeye

The E-2 Hawkeye is probably the most important aircraft in the Navy fleet; it is "The Eyes of the Fleet."

It is the first player when starting a NO FLY ZONE and establishing AIR SUPERIORITY.

In combat, whoever sees the enemy first wins!

The E-2 Hawkeye is an AIRBORNE EARLY WARNING aircraft and has a powerful AN/APY-9 radar which enables it to track more than 2,000 targets simultaneously at a range of more than 400 miles, and at the same time guide 40 to 100 air-to-air intercepts or air-to-surface engagements.

It's no wonder the E-2 Hawkeye is called a "Flying Command Post!"

Northrop Grumman EA-6B Prowler

The EA-6B Prowler is an ELECTRONIC WARFARE AIRCRAFT.

That means its primary role is to jam enemy radar, on the ground and in the air.

Jamming enemies' radar is also called ELECTRONIC COUNTERMEASURES or ECM.

Like the E2 Hawkeye, the Prowler is one of the first aircraft in a battlezone. The Prowler then jams the enemy radars on the ground and in enemy aircraft. This way the attack aircraft like the F/A-18 can fly their mission without being hit by enemy anti-aircraft missiles.

The EA-6B Prowler can also fire ARM missiles. "ARM" means **A**nti **R**adiation **M**issile; which is just a fancy way of saying "radar killer!"

The EA-6B Prowler served in the US Navy until 2015 and is now being replaced by the…

Boeing EA-18G Growler

The EA-18G Growler is based on the F/A-18 two seater version of the Super Hornet.

You can see the ECM Pods on the wingtips of this EA-18 Growler as it takes off. Under the wing is the AN/ALQ-99 Jamming Pod.

The Growler can fly higher, faster, and farther, and carry more weapons and Electronic Warfare devices than the EA-6B Prowler. It is also equipped with the newest radars and radar jamming equipment.

RESCUE AND MULTI-ROLE AIRCRAFT

Sikorsky CH-53E Super Stallion / MH-53 Sea Dragon

The Sikorsky CH-53 is the HEAVY LIFTER of the Navy and it is the largest helicopter in the United States military.

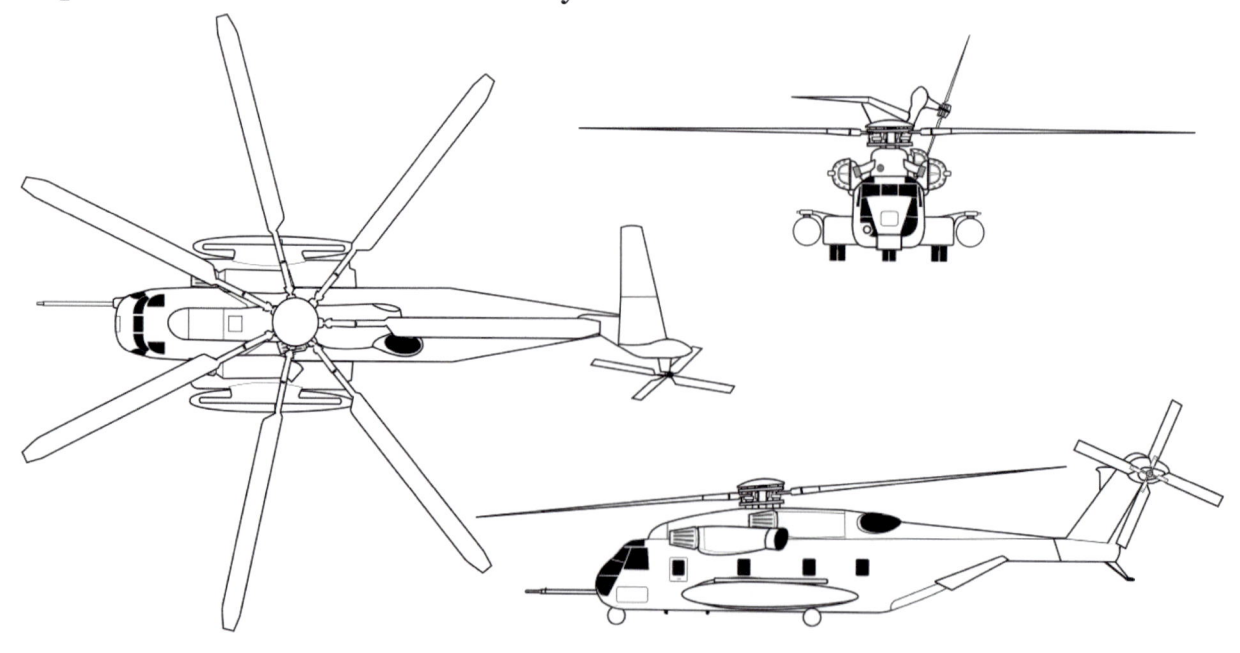

Sikorsky SH-60 Seahawk

The Seahawk is based on the UH-60 Blackhawk. It is the primary SEARCH AND RESCUE helicopter of the United States Navy. Equally important, it also performs anti-submarine warfare; which means it's a SUB HUNTER!

The enemy is ABOVE and BELOW the surface!

US NAVY

Besides Search and Rescue, and Submarine Hunting, the Seahawk can also attack targets:

An MH-60R Seahawk fires an AGM-65 Hellfire missile

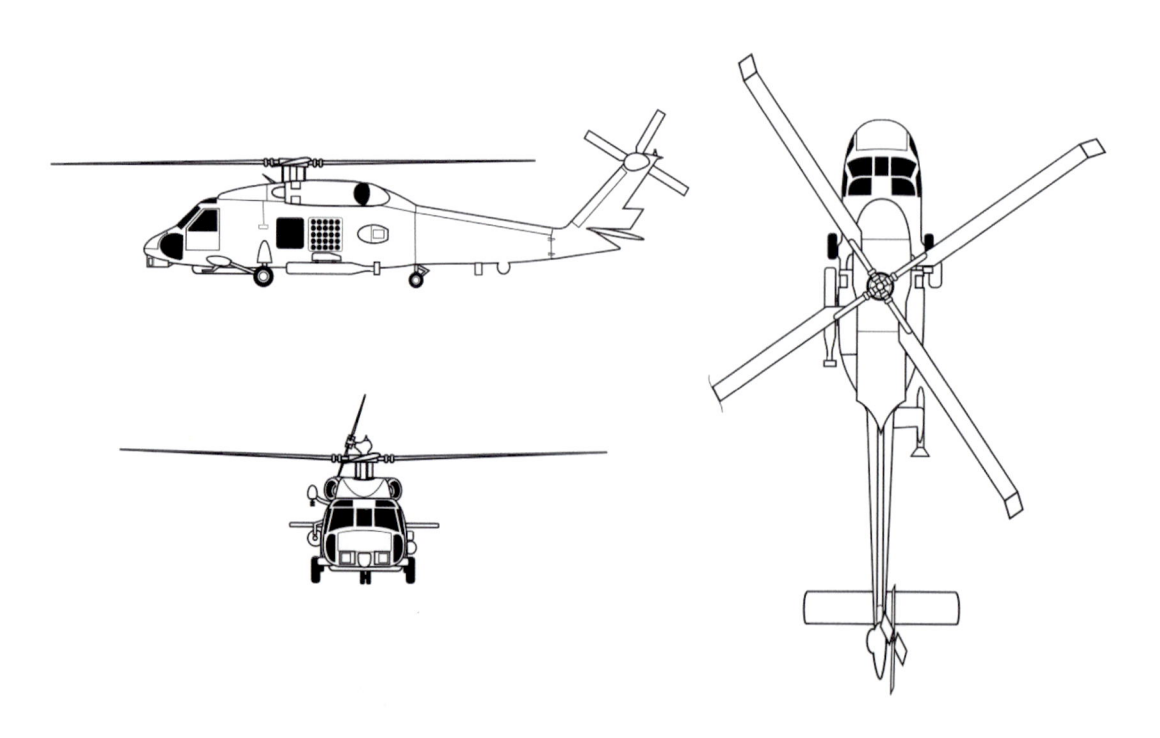

62

The End

I hope you enjoyed this book and are on your way to becoming a Naval Aviator now.

Thank you for buying and reading this book and trusting me to offer something of value.

If you liked this book you may like the others at:

www.thekidsbooks.blogspot.com

You can also see my other books and author profile on Amazon here:

www.amazon.com/author/ericz

Here's to your success!

Your Free Gift

Get the Blue Angels Aerobatics for FREE

When you join The Kids Books!
Just Go type this into any web browser:

bit.ly/aeroGift

Made in the USA
Columbia, SC
05 July 2025